ALL-NEW FIR

USER MANUAL

The Illustrated, Practical Guide with Tips & Tricks to

Master Your 2019 Kindle Fire 7 Tablet

Raphael Stone

i

CONTENTS

Introduction

The Amazon Fire tablet range continues to rise in popularity, gaining ground in what is described as a "declining market". Is it all about the price?

The Fire 7 is a fairly chunky tablet finished in matte plastic, which curves into the 7-inch screen. It is the perfect size for portability. It's is comfortable to hold with one hand and easy to stow in a bag.

The latest Amazon Fire 7 (2019) features a faster quad-core processor, 2× the storage, hands-free with Alexa, and 2× as durable as the latest iPad mini.

You can use the Fire 7 to enjoy movies, TV episodes, games, apps, ebooks, and songs. Alexa can connect you to the information, entertainment, and people who matter most – with just your voice. Ask to play videos and music, open apps, shop online, check weather, call or message almost anyone and much more.

Just say "Alexa" – even when the tablet screen is on standby.

This book is a beginner to expert guide that will teach you all the tips and tricks that you need to make the most of your Fire 7 tablet.

How to setup Fire 7 tablet

If you've just received the Fire 7 tablet or bought one for yourself, here's how to get it up and running. We'll explain how to associate it with your Amazon account. Usually, there will be enough battery power to get through the setup process and install a few apps. But it's also a good idea to attach the bundled USB cable and mains charger and allow the battery to fully charge for an hour or two first.

When you turn on a Fire tablet for the first time, it will ask to choose a language and a region.

Tap Continue and you'll see the Connect to Wi-Fi screen. The password for your Wi-Fi network is usually on a sticker on your router, or sometimes on a removable card.

Choose the correct network name from the list and type the password, which will be case-sensitive, so make sure you match CAPITAL and lowercase letters. The tablet will check if there are any software updates, download and then install them.

Next, you'll be prompted to enter your Amazon account details to register the tablet: email address and password. This is necessary in the same way it is on a Google or Apple phone: you can't install any apps or games or any other content from Amazon (such as books, videos and more) without an Amazon account.

Signing in with an Amazon account will also allow you to install apps from any web browser, rather than on the tablet itself. (You'll need to go to www.amazon.com or www.amazon.co.uk and sign in with the same Amazon account, then search for the app to see the option to install it on your tablet.)

If you don't have an Amazon account, you can tap the 'New to Amazon' link to create an account. If you've had a Fire tablet before, you may be offered the option to restore a backup. You can restore the most recent backup to save the hassle of installing apps and games. Plus all your settings will be as you set them, including email accounts, bookmarks and more.

On the next screen you can opt in (or out) of location services, and backing up your stuff to Amazon. It's well worth enabling Backup & Restore to make it easy to swap to a new Amazon tablet should you need to.

Then you'll be prompted to select which members of your Amazon Household will use the tablet. This streamlines the creation of user profiles, but you'll only see them if you've previously set them up on your Amazon account.

If not, you will see the option to add a child account. A child account has a completely different interface to an adult profile and limits what they can see and do. It also gives them access (if you allow it) to a kid-safe web browser. To learn more, also read on How to set up parental controls on a Fire tablet.

Next you can link other social accounts, if you want to, and then you'll see an adverts for Audible audiobooks and Kindle Unlimited. Either tap No Thanks or 'Start My Free Trial'.

How to name your Fire tablet

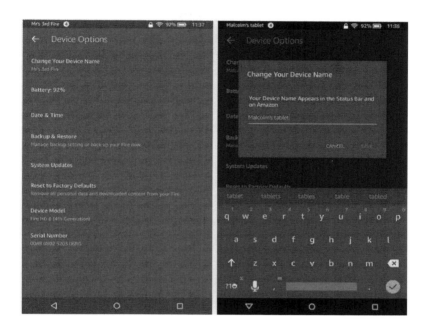

If you use a number of different devices with your Amazon account, then things can quickly get confusing. Why not pick a descriptive name for your Fire tablet, rather than sticking with "Mr's 3rd Fire"? All you have to do to change the name of your Fire tablet is pull down the notification shade from the top and tap **Settings > Device Options > Change Your Device Name**.

How to Create A Child Profile

Whether you bought a Fire tablet just for your child to use, or you want to be able to hand your own Fire to your child once in a while, a Child Profile is essential for keeping kids away from your media, apps, and settings.

It's also great for sharing select media with a child, or sharing one Kindle Fire with multiple children of different ages. Creating a Child Profile is easy and can be done in just a minute or two. Once the profile is set up, if you want to, you can go deeper into the settings and get very specific.

Initial Setup:

1. Swipe down from the top of the Fire's screen.

2. Press Settings.

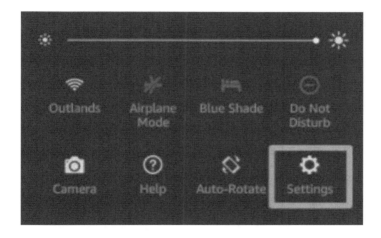

3. Scroll down to the "Personal" section and
press Profiles & Family Library.

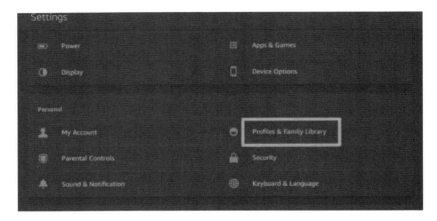

4. Press Add a child profile.

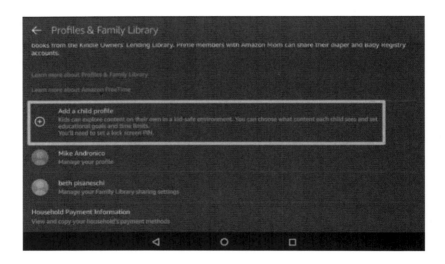

5. Note that if you don't already have a lockscreen passcode set up for your profile, you will be prompted to set one up. This is so your kids can't use your account.

6. Select PIN or Password,

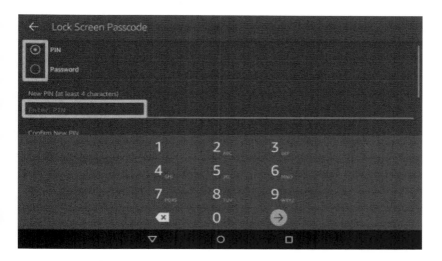

7. Re-enter the PIN or Password, and tap Finish.

8.   Enter   the   child's   first   name   where prompted. Press Choose a profile picture if you would like to do that at this time.

9. Tap Boy to select a gender and tap Birthdate to enter their date of birth.

10. Choose either Use Amazon FreeTime or Use Teen Profiles, and then tap Add Profile. The Fire will preselect one for you based on the child's birth date, but you can change it. (Teen Profiles have a less child-like look, but you will still have access to the same settings.)

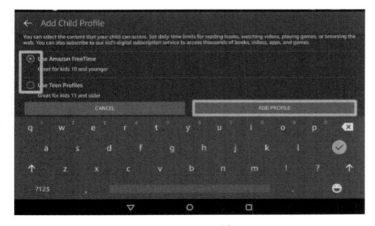

11. You will then be taken to a screen that lets you add content from your own collection to that profile. Tap Done when you're finished. The first tab is labeled Kid Friendly. This is the Amazon content you already own that is designated as appropriate for children. You can click on Add All Kids' Titles or click on individual titles. You can also click on the other tabs (Books, Videos, and Games & Apps) and choose individual titles. Titles with a check mark will be accessible from the child's profile.

12. If you're not already a member, you'll get a prompt to sign up for FreeTime Unlimited, which starts at $2.99 per month after a 1 month free trial. Select Start Free Trial or No Thanks.

13. Tap Enable Browser to get the FreeTime Web Browser, which only lets kids view content that Amazon believes to be age-appropriate.

14. Check the boxes next to child profiles to give browser access rights, and tap Done.

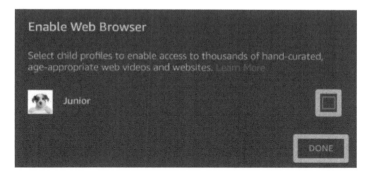

15. Tap OK to recognize that the Fire tablet uses filters to decide which web pages and FreeTime Unlimited content is appropriate.

16. The child profile is now ready to be used. You can turn the Enable Web Browser switch off to take this privilege away from your child.

The rest of the settings can be accessed from the child's profile settings screen. Swipe down from the top of the Kindle Fire's home screen and press Settings. Scroll down to the Personal section and press Profiles & Family Library. Press the profile that you'd like to manage to access the following settings. Note that if you are already in the child's profile, swiping down and pressing Settings will get you to that profile's passcode-protected settings screen – you do not need to go back to your own profile.

Child Settings

1. Press Set Daily Goals & Time Limits (if Daily Goals & Time Limits is set to off, move slider to the right to turn on).

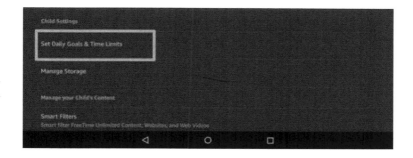

2. Set bedtime times, which regulate the window of time this profile will not be accessible during. Tabs at the top are used to move between settings for Weekdays and Weekends.

3. Set Education Goals for your child to meet each day. If you check the Learn First box, your child will not be able to access other content on the Fire until these goals are met. For the purpose of these goals, Amazon labels individual videos, apps, and games as either "educational" or "entertainment." All books are labeled as "educational," and all web browsing is labeled as "entertainment."

4. Select Total Screen Time, or Time by Activity, to decide how you want to limit usage. If you choose Time by Activity, you'll break the allotment down by books, videos and apps.

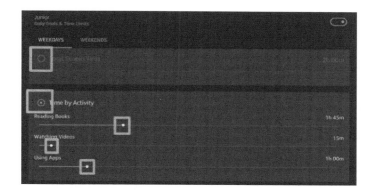

If you don't want to set a screen time limit, choose Total Screen Time and drag the slider all the way to the right, until it says "Unlimited."

5. Press Manage Storage to see how much storage is free on your device.

6. If your kid's data is taking up too much space, tap on their profile to clear its data. If you're running low on storage, press Archive Now to free up space. To see what is available

for archiving, press View Contents. To see how your storage is being used, press either Internal Storage or (if you have one installed) the SD card.

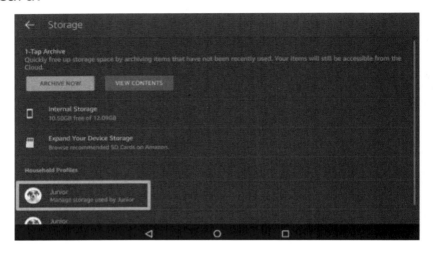

Manage your Child's Content

1. Press Smart Filters.

2. Drag both ends of the age range slider to determine what FreeTime Unlimited content and websites your child has access to. (These filters do not affect titles that you've added to your child's profile from your own library.) Move the left and right sides of the filter slider to highlight the ages of the content you would like included on the child's profile. As you move the slider you can see examples of appropriate titles under the slider.

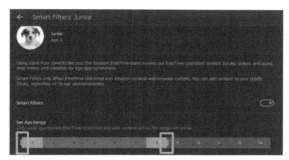

3. **Press Add Content.**

4. Here, choose the tab of the content you would like to add (Kid Friendly, Books, Videos, Games & Apps), and select content from your library to share with your child. If you have enabled the web browser there will be addition choices that will be discussed in the Web Settings section below. For Books, Videos, or Games & Apps, press each title to toggle the check mark – titles with a check mark will be included in the child's profile. Press Done to save any changes.

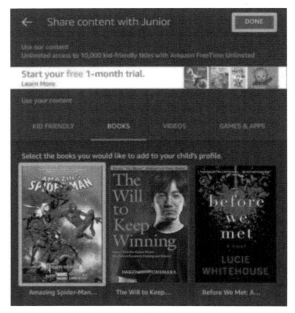

5. If you would like to remove content, press **Remove Content.**

6. Choose content to remove, and tap **Done**.

7. Unwanted FreeTime Unlimited items can be removed by searching for individual titles that you want to block, or by browsing through all available items (there is a dropdown to enable browsing by Books, Videos, or Apps, or to see a list of blocked content). Pressing an individual title will block it (there will be a lock icon in front of it), and pressing it again will make it available to the child's profile (no lock icon).

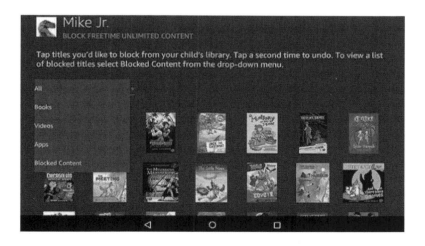

8. If you have enabled the Web Browser you can tap **Limit Web Content**.

9. Then, choose either Websites or Web Videos, where you manage the content available to this profile. Here, you can also turn off activity-tracking Cookies, and disable or enable Amazon's web curation.

10. **Press the + sign.**

11. **Enter a web address or the name of a video** if you're adding web video.

12. Tap **Allow**.

13. Tap **Done** to move on, or next to add another.

14. Press View Your Child's Web History to see a complete list of every website and video your child visited or attempted to visit. (If "History has not been synchronized" is displayed, press the circular arrows to the right.)

15. Press either the Visited tab or the Attempted tab, and then press Review to check out the website in question; while there you can choose to Allow or Block it.

16. If you would like your child to be able to make in-app purchases, move the slider to the right next to Enable In-App Purchasing. Even with this setting turned on, your child will still need the Amazon account's password in order to make an in-app purchase. If you do not already have 1-click Ordering set up on your Amazon account, you will be prompted to do so.

17. Tap **Enable**.

FreeTime Unlimited

If you have a FreeTime Unlimited subscription, you can choose which child profiles have access to the content.

1. Press **Manage Your Subscription**.

2. **Manage Your Plan**.

3. Check the boxes for the child profiles that you would like to have access to the FreeTime Unlimited content, and press Save.

Camera Settings

1. To turn camera access off and on for an account, toggle the switch next to Enable Camera & Photo Gallery.

2. To change the Prime Photos storage settings, press Auto-Save Settings for Photos & Videos.

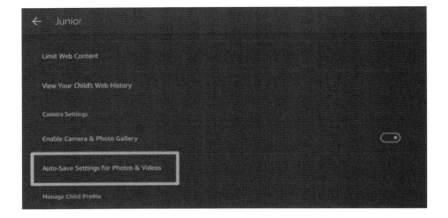

3. Check the box next to each child's profile whose camera images you would like to automatically save to the cloud.

Manage Child Profile

1. Press **Edit Child Profile** to change the basic settings from the first steps of setting up a Child Profile. You can change the name, gender, birthday, and profile picture, or switch profile type (FreeTime or Teen)

2. Press **Remove Child Profile** ONLY if you want to completely remove a child from the Fire.

3. Tap **Remove Profile** to confirm.

General Settings

1. If you would like to temporarily hide a child's profile from the lock screen (meaning that the child will not be able to use the profile), move the slider to the left next to Show Profile on Lock Screen.

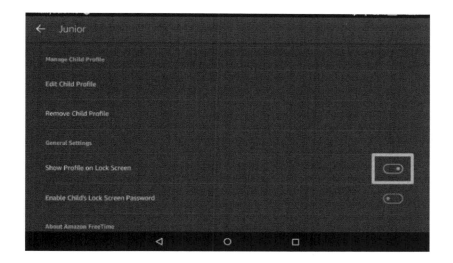

2. You will still be to see the child's profile in the settings, and can turn the profile back on at any time. Pressing **Enable Child's Lock Screen Password** will allow you to set up a PIN or Password for a child's profile.

3. This can be useful if more than one child shares a Fire and you don't want them to be able to access each other's profiles. Enter the PIN or Password, enter it again to confirm, and press Finish.

How to Configure Parental Controls

Kindle Fire tablets have the built-in ability to password-protect or block different features of the tablet without having to set up a separate profile, enabling you to hand your Fire over to a child or someone you don't necessarily want to give full access to. You can password-protect things like Prime Video, email, and Amazon purchasing, and turn the controls off whenever you want.

When Parental Controls are on you'll see a little lock icon at the top of the Fire's screen. If you swipe down from the top, you'll see a message that says "Parental Controls – On." You can tap that message at any time to enter the Parental

Controls password and turn the controls off. Note that while some controls carry over to Child Profiles, not all of them do. Parental Controls are much better at locking down adult content on Adult Profiles than blocking allowed content on Child Profiles.

1. Swipe down from the top of the screen.

2. Press **Settings**.

3. Under **Personal**, press **Parental Controls**.

4. Move the Parental Controls slider to the right to turn Parental Controls on.

5. Depending on whether you've set up Parental Controls before, you may be asked for your Parental Controls password, or be prompted to set up a new password. Note that this is different from your Lockscreen password.

6. Select **Amazon Content and Apps**.

7. On the next screen, you can block or unblock

Newsstand (newspaper, magazine, and blog subscriptions) Books, Audible, Music, Amazon Video, Docs, Apps & Games, Photos, Web Browser, Email, Contacts, Calendars, Camera, and Amazon Maps. Alexa cannot be unblocked as long as Parental Controls are on.

8. Press **Password Protection**.

9. On the next screen you can turn on or off password protection for Video and Twitch Playback, Wi-Fi, and Location Services. These services will all be operable, but you'll need to enter the Parental Controls password to turn them on.

10. Press **Amazon Stores (excluding Video)** to block or unblock access to Amazon, except for Amazon Videos. If you want to block video playback, use Password Protection (above). If you want to block video purchases, press Password Protect Purchases, which will require a password to buy or download anything from Amazon.

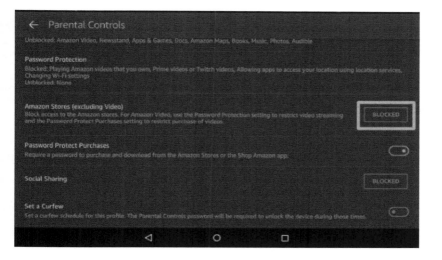

11. Press **Social Sharing** to block or unblock social sharing apps like Twitter and Facebook.

12. Turn on **Set a Curfew** to enable a Curfew Schedule.

13. Tap **Curfew Schedule**. Note that signing into the Fire during a curfew will set the curfew to "off." It must be set to "on" again to enable the curfew feature.

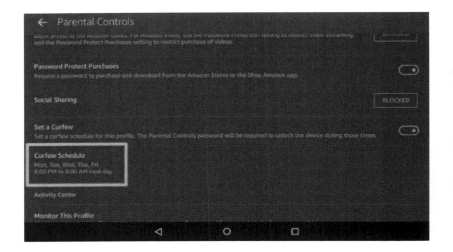

14. Tap Days, Start Time and End Time to adjust the Curfew limits.

15. Press **Monitor this Profile**, which allows you to view detailed information about which apps and games were used and for how long, exactly what music, video, and book titles were accessed, and much more. Once Monitor This Profile has been turned on, you will see a little parent/child icon at the top of the screen, and if you swipe down from the top you will see a message that says "Monitoring – On."

16. You can access the information it gathers by visiting www.amazon.com/mycd and clicking on "Your Devices." Note that Monitor This Profile can only be turned on for the parent profile controlling the Parental Controls, not for child profiles.

How to Install a VPN on Kindle Fire

The Kindle Fire is locked to the Amazon store. Amazon doesn't let consumers buy software from the Google Play app store. This restriction makes it very difficult to get content onto a

Kindle device (other than the stuff that Amazon provides). Luckily, it is possible to sideload apps onto a Kindle Fire.

While it is true that until recently Amazon didn't have VPNs on its store - now it does have some (ExpressVPN, PureVPN, IPVanish, PrivateVPN, to name a few). However, if you subscribe to a VPN for Kindle that does not have software in the store, you can still use the VPN by installing third-party OpenVPN software onto your Kindle. Once that is installed you can configure the OpenVPN software to work with your chosen VPN provider. We will explain how to do it later in this guide.

If you are worried that any of this sounds complicated - relax - because it isn't. What's more, whichever VPN you subscribe to will have a setup guide to help you with the process! However, if you are concerned about this - you can always communicate with the VPN directly before you purchase a subscription to get some peace of mind and ensure that you are going to get all the help you need.

If this is something you do not want to have to deal with, we recommend having a quick search for the VPN you are interested in on the Amazon store before you go the trouble of subscribing. If the VPN has software on the Amazon store, then you can follow these simple steps:

- Subscribe to your preferred VPN for Kindle
- Go to the Amazon store and download the VPN software
- Run the software and log in with your credentials
- Connect to a VPN server and begin accessing previously blocked content.

To help you out, let's also take a look at how to set up a VPN using third party OpenVPN for Kindle. If you decide to go for the most complicated method of using a VPN on Kindle (because you prefer to use a VPN that doesn't have software on the Amazon App store) then follow these steps:

1. Drag the Kindle notification bar down. Select More followed by Device and turn on "Allow Installation of Applications from unknown sources."

2. Download ES File Explorer from the Amazon Appstore. This app is free.

3. Download the OpenVPN installer to your desktop computer.

4. Connect your Kindle to your PC or Mac using the USB lead, then drag and drop the OpenVPN installer (icsopenvpn0529.apk) to your Kindle's Downloads folder.

5. Start up your Kindle and use ES Explorer to navigate to the Downloads folder. Tap on the .apk file and install it.

6. Sign up for a VPN service for Kindle if you haven't already done so.

7. Next set up the OpenVPN software on your Kindle with your VPN's OpenVPN config files. These files will be supplied by your VPN provider. To get them onto your Kindle you will need to download them to a PC, unzip them, and email them to yourself. Open the email on your Kindle and download the vpn files. Now you can import them from your downloads folder into the OpenVPN software. Your VPN will have a setup guide to help you with this step!

How to Stop Amazon In-App Purchases

The FTC and tons of parents are hopping mad at Amazon for allowing millions of dollars worth of unauthorized in-app purchases to go through. The FTC even filed a complaint in a U.S. District court to say so. The federal agency is demanding the e-tailer refund parents the 30 percent of in-app purchases that it keeps (the rest goes to the app maker).

Amazon's policy is not to give refunds, and Apple once held a similar policy. But following an FTC degree earlier last year, customers were sent directions for how to apply for a refund.

In March 2012, Amazon updated its in-app charge system to require a password for charges larger than $20. But it's remarkably easy to stop your kids from making any purchases. In fact, it's a simple five-step process on the Kindle Fire HDX.

1. Slide your finger down from the top of the screen.

2. Tap **Settings**.

3. Tap **Parental Controls**.

4. Toggle on **Parental Controls**.

5. Enter your password and tap **Submit.**

6.   Double check   that   **Password   Protect Purchases** is toggled On.

That's it; literally five steps. This will ensure that kids can't download new apps or make in-app purchases. Among other things you can restrict in the Kindle Parental Controls section is blocking games, social sharing, Web browsing and email.

Disable In-App Purchases on Amazon Appstore

If you own a non-Kindle Android device and want to disable in-app purchases, here's what you need to do.

1. Open the **Amazon App Store.**

2. Tap the **menu button** of three lines on the

top left.

3. Tap **Settings**.

4. Select **In-App Purchasing.**

5. Uncheck the box. You'll be asked to enter your password. Then click **Continue**.

Checking Out Books and Purchasing them on the Kindle Store

Here I am going to show you how to download a book. I will make the steps as precise as possible in this section.

First, you need to log into your Amazon account, which is the first thing that happens when you turn on the fire for the first time. If you don't have one, sign up. In your Amazon account you need to make sure that you check the box for **"One-click purchases**," otherwise purchases won't work in your Fire HD. After you do that, you can go ahead and download a book. Click on "**store**" and allow it connect to the Amazon store – tap in the search bar and type the genre of the book you wish to purchase.

If you know the exact book that you want, you can just type in the title or the name of the author and click "Go". Several books would be displayed with their prices by the side, a lot of them are free. When you type the name of your favorite author, it lists all the books by the author. You can also search for book on the New York Times Best Sellers list by typing "**New York Times Best Sellers**" in the search bar, then tap on "**Go**". And you will get a list of current best sellers.

To search for all free books, type the word "**Free**" in the search bar and all the books that are free in the store would be listed out for you to choose which to download into your Kindle device. You can go ahead and pick any of the books you want and click on "Buy for free" and the book would be downloaded into your Kindle device. You can change the character size to something big or small depending on the condition of your eyes. If the book isn't free, you would need to purchase it using your credit card.

How to Email Books and Documents to Kindle?

Besides transfer eBooks and documents to Kindle via USB cable, or sync your purchased books to Kindle directly through WIFI or 3G, Amazon also provides a free tool called Kindle Personal Documents Service which allows you to send personal eBooks and documents to Kindle by Email. The service is compatiable with Kindle eReader (such as Kindle Paperwhite, Kindle Voyage), Kindle Fire, and even Kindle reading app.

But how do you email books and documents to Kindle? You may think it's pretty easy, but before you use it, you need to find your Send to

Kindle Email address, and add it to your approved email list. If you are not familiar with it, follow in details. I will show you how to do it, and also share some useful tips & tricks when email files to Kindle, such as how to send epub books to Kindle by Email, and how to convert PDF to Kindle format when send by Email.

Supported File Types When Send to Kindle by Email

Kindle Personal Documents Service supports the following file types:

- Kindle Format (.MOBI, .AZW)
- Microsoft Word (.DOC, .DOCX)
- HTML (.HTML, .HTM)
- RTF (.RTF)
- Text (.TXT)
- JPEG (.JPEG, .JPG)
- GIF (.GIF)
- PNG (.PNG)
- BMP (.BMP)
- PDF (.PDF)

Please take note that the file size must be under 50MB. And Amazon also limit the number of documents you send or store, but they don't say the exact quantity, I think it's enough for personal use. Follow these steps to send document via email to your Kindle.

1. Find Your Kindle Personal Email Address

When I surf on internet, I found there are many people don't know their Kindle email address, Infact, you can find your Kindle personal email address on Kindle eReader or Amazon website. To find Kindle Personal Email Address on eReader:

Tap "*Settings*" --> "*Device options*" --> "*Personalize your Kindle*" --> "*Send-to-Kindle Email*"

To find Kindle Personal Email Address on Amazon website:

Go to Amazon website, find "**Manage Your Content and Devices**". Click "**Your Devices**", and you will see all your Kindle devices, including your Kindle Reading App, such as Kindle for android, Kindle for iOS. Click the device or app you want, and you will see the Kindle personal email address. Normally, it ends with @kindle.com.

2. Kindle-personal email address

Add Your Email to "Send to Kindle" Approved Email list. To prevent spam, Kindle Personal Documents Service only accept email which approved by yourself, so you need to add your personal email address.

Go to Amazon Manage Your Content and Devices. From Settings column, scroll down to Personal Document Settings. Under Send-to-Kindle Email Settings, your Send to Kindle email address will be listed. Click "Add a new approved e-mail address", enter a new email address, and then click Save to save your changes.

3. Add email to Kindle

Notice: If you want to save your personal ebooks and documents to Kindle account, don't forget to enable archive, just simply click "Edit Archive Settings".

4. Compose an Email and Attached Your Books or Documents

- Log in your approved email account, compose a new email.

- Recipient is "xxx@kindle.com" which can be found on Kindle eReader and Amazon Website.

- Leave the subject and content as blank or write whatever you like.

Tips: If you want to convert PDF or txt to the Kindle compatible format, type "convert" in the subject when e-mailing a personal document to your Send-to-Kindle address.

- Upload your personal books and documents, and then click "send".

Email Books and Documents to Kindle from

Calibre

If you use Calibre to manage your books, you can also email your books and documents from Calibre. Go to Perference >> Sharing books by email to set up the email address.

sharing books by email

Next time, when you want to email a book or document to Kindle directly from Calibre, you just need to right click the title and find Connect/share >> Email to xxx@kindle.com. Then the title will be delivery to your Kindle device or app.

Send ePub books to Kindle by Email

As we know, Kindle don't support epub format, so if we want to read epub books on Kindle, we need convert epub to Kindle azw or mobi format first. But if you send epub books to Kindle by email, you don't need to do this. There are two method to send ePub books to Kindle by Email directly.

Method 1: If you email books and documents

to Kindle from Calibre, Calibre will automatically convert it to Kindle format, it's very convenient.

Method 2: Change the EPUB book's suffix from .epub to .zip, and send the zip file to Kindle by email, Kindle Personal Documents Service will convert the zip file to azw format automatically.

How To Transfer Books to Kindle, Kindle Fire and Kindle App

Kindle Paperwhite People can read Amazon Kindle books on Kindle eReaders, Kindle Fire tablets as well as other smart devices with Kindle apps installed. Generally, once a device is registered to an Amazon account, all Kindle books under that account will be synced automatically with Internet connected.

However, if we want to read non-Amazon books on Kindle or purchased Kindle books do not shown on the device due to a connection problem, we will have to transfer books from computer to Kindle manually. This guide will tell you how to transfer books to Kindle, Kindle Fire (HD), Kindle Paperwhite, Kindle for Android/iPad app from PC or Mac.

Step 1: Make sure your personal books are MOBI format.

Amazon Kindle does not support EPUB books, but supports MOBI (DRM-free) and PDF formats. I personally prefer MOBI to PDF because the former is more flexible and better for reading.

Books downloaded from torrent sites are often EPUB or PDF. If you want to transfer these books to Kindle for reading, you will have to convert them to Kindle supported MOBI or PDF.

If you want to transfer eBooks purchased from Barnes & Noble, Kobo, Sony or other stores to Kindle, things will be a little tough. These books are typically DRM protected so we can't directly convert the formats. Instead, we have to strip the DRM restrictions first. DRM-protected PDF books also have to be decrypted because Kindle only supports DRM-free PDF. You will need to download DRM Removal tool in order to do that.

Step 2: Transfer books to Kindle, Kindle Fire(HD) and Kindle apps from computer

Once the books are open MOBI or PDF, we can easily transfer them from PC/Mac to Kindle, Paperwhite, Kindle Fire (HD), Kindle for Android / iPad app with USB or wirelessly.

To transfer books to Kindle:

- Connect your device to computer via USB.
- Double click the drive to open it and view the folders.
- Select the item you want to transfer (mobi or pdf).
- Copy books to the folder (documents) under Kindle drive.
- Or you can also use the Send-to-Kindle email address.

How to Transfer MOBI/PDF books to Kindle, Kindle Paperwhite and other Kindle E-ink readers

1. Connect the Kindle device to computer with the USB cable. It will be recognized as a "Kindle" drive.

2. Drag and drop the MOBI books to the "documents" folder under Kindle drive.

3. Eject Kindle from computer. The loaded books will display under "Device" shelf.

Send-to-Kindle E-mail Address

Tap the menu icon (top right corner) from the home screen, then "Settings" -> "Device Options" -> "Personalize your Kindle" -> "Send-to-Kindle E-mail"

For conventional Kindle, select "Settings" from the home screen menu and use the Next page and Previous Page buttons to get the Send-to-Kindle E-mail.

Transfer MOBI/PDF books to Kindle Fire and Kindle Fire HD

Note that Kindle Fire (HD) does not come with a USB cable. If you don't have a USB cable, get the Send-to-Kindle email address of the Kindle

Fire and transfer MOBI or PDF books to it wirelessly. Here I take the Kindle Fire for example.

- Connect your Kindle Fire (HD) to computer with the USB cable and it will be recognized as a Kindle drive.
- Copy and paste your MOBI books to the "Books" folder under the Kindle Fire (HD) Drive.
- copy books to Kindle Fire HD
- Check the transferred books by tapping "Books" (on the top menu bar) then "Device".

Send-to-Kindle E-mail Address of Kindle Fire:

Tap the top right corner, select "More..." -> "My Account" to get the device email address.

Transfer MOBI/PDF books to Kindle for Android app

Here I take the Nexus 7 for example.

- Connect your Android tablet or smart phone to PC.

- Go to the "Kindle" folder of your Android device storage. Copy and paste the MOBI books to that folder.

- Tap the menu icon in the top right corner of Kindle app, then select "On Device" to check the transferred books.

Send-to-Kindle E-mail Address of Kindle for Android app:

Tap the menu icon (top left corner), then "Setting" to get the "Send-to-Kindle E-mail Address".

Transfer MOBI/PDF books to iPad / iPod / iPhone Kindle app

There is no way to directly transfer MOBI books to Kindle iPad / iPod / iPhone app with iTunes. In this case, we can use Kindle email system to send personal MOBI books to the email address of Kindle for iPad app. PDF files can be transferred to iPad with iTunes (opened with iBooks by default) or with Kindle for iPad email address (opened with Kindle for iPad app by default).

Send-to-Kindle E-mail Address of Kindle for iPad app:

Tap the gear icon in the bottom right corner and select "Send-to-Kindle Email Address".

Transfer MOBI/PDF books to Kindle wirelessly (without a USB cable)

As long as we know the email addresses of the Kindle devices or apps, we will be able to send DRM-free MOBI and PDF books to Kindle, Kindle Paperwhite, Kindle Fire (HD), Kindle for Android / iPad app wirelessly.

1. Add your own (sender) email address to Kindle Approved Personal Document E-mail List.

Visit Manage Your Kindle to sign in, go to "Your Kindle Account" from the left side menu and select "Personal Document Settings". Pay attention to the "Approved Personal Document E-mail List" and select "Add a new approved email address." Enter your e-mail address then click "Add Address."

2. Compose an empty email (empty subject and empty body), attach your MOBI or PDF docs and input the Send-to-Kindle E-mail address to send.

Tap sync icon on the Kindle device or Kindle app. In minutes, you will find the sent MOBI and PDF docs under "All Items" and "Docs" category (Cloud).

Note: When you transfer PDF books to Kindle from computer, you will find the books not shown under "Books" (on device) shelf or category. That's right. PDF books typically display under "Docs" (on device) shelf.

If your purchased Kindle books are not auto synced due to an Internet issue, you can download the books to your computer (Amazon site -> "Manage Your Kindle" under "Your Account" -> "Actions..." -> "Deliver to my..." -> "Download and transfer via USB") to download the books to your computer. The downloaded books are typically AZW3. Transfer them to your Kindle device or app according to steps above.

This guide is based on Windows OS, but it also works if you want to transfer books to Kindle from Mac. As long as the books are not protected and converted to Kindle supported formats (MOBI or PDF), we will be able to read eBooks from other sources without confining to Amazon.

How to Turn Off Ads on Fire Tablets

Amazon allows Fire tablet shoppers to save $15 at checkout, in exchange for allowing the mega retailer to place ads (which Amazon coyly calls "special offers") on the home screens of said slates. But we're guessing that you're tired of seeing these ads, and want to free your tablet from the experience.

In order to do so, you'll need to follow the below steps to pull up Amazon's website, opt out, and pay Amazon the $15 you saved up front. Here's how to disable ads on your Amazon Fire Tablet.

1. Navigate to **amazon.com.**

2. Hover over **Account & Lists.**

3. Select **Your Content and Devices** under Your Account.

4. Click **Your Devices**.

5. Click the ... next to your device.
6. Click **Edit under Special Offers**.

7. In the next window, you'll get the option to pay $15 to disable Special Offers and Ads.

8. On your Fire tablet, swipe down from the top of the screen.

9. Tap **Settings**.

10. Tap **Apps & Games.**

11. Tap **Amazon Application Settings.**

12. Tap **Home Screens**.

13. Turn off the **Recommendations** option. You've disabled ads for an Amazon Fire tablet!

How to uninstall apps

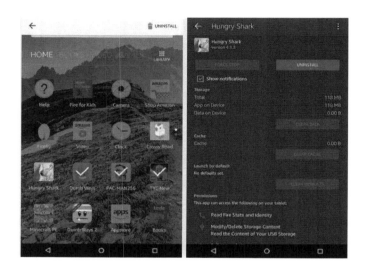

You generally tap and hold on an app, or another piece of content, if you want to remove it from your Fire tablet. If you're in the carousel, then you should get the pop-up option to remove or uninstall whatever you've long pressed on.

If you're on the home screen, then you can tap and hold on an app icon to get the Uninstall option to appear in the top right. Now, you can tap to select multiple apps and then tap Uninstall to get rid of all of them at once.

You can also uninstall apps or games one by one by going to **Settings** > **Apps & Games** > **Manage All Applications**. Tap on the app you want to get rid of, and then tap Uninstall in the top right.

How to change your wallpaper

If you'd like to change the background image on your home screen, then you need to choose a new wallpaper. To do so, go to **Settings** > **Display** > **Wallpaper**. You'll see a few options here, but you can also tap Pick image to use one of your own photos as your wallpaper.

How to manage notifications

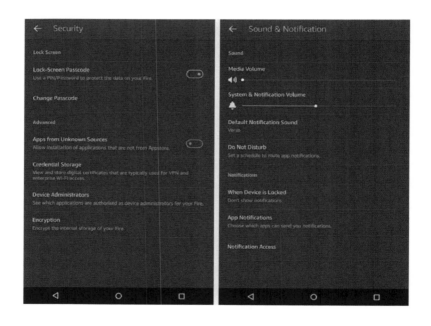

Some apps on your Fire tablet will send you notifications that pop up in the notification shade. That can be useful when you have an incoming email or there's an update worth downloading, but sometimes you'll get notifications that you simply have no interest in receiving.

If you find that a particular app or game is sending you too many pointless notifications, then you should turn them off. You can do so by going to Settings > Sound & Notification > App Notifications. Tap on the app in question and you can block notifications completely. Conversely, if there's an app you always want to hear from, toggle Priority on and the app's notifications will always appear at the top of your notification shade.

How to Share Kindle Fire Books with Friends

When you purchased a nice eBook in Amazon Store, you are hooked immediately by this book and want to share it with your family or your best friends after you finish reading it without a break.

Oops, problem here. You cannot share it with your family or friends! Because the book has DRM protection, they can only be read on your Kindle. Relax, here we introduce you 4 methods to share Kindle books.

1. Use a Kindle DRM Removal to break the limitation;
2. Share Kindle books in the same account;
3. Share Kindle books by lending out;
4. Share Kindle books by Kindle Family Library.

Method 1: Share books on kindle fire by removing Kindle DRM

Download and install **Kindle DRM Removal**. It helps you remove DRM from Kindle books, then you can copy your books to anywhere (for personal use please).

Method 2: Share Kindle Fire ebooks with the same account

Before you choose this method, please make sure the people you want to share the book with are very close to you. As we know, an Amazon account can be authorized on 6 Kindle devices, which is the base of this method.

- 1 Your friend should de-register his Kindle.
- 2 Tell your Kindle ID & Password to your friend.
- 3 Your friend register his/her Kindle with your ID
- 4 Your books will show up on your friend's cloud, and he/she can sync the books now.

Attention: Turn off the Whispersync Device Synchronization (whispersync for Kindle) if you are sharing Kindle books on different devices with the same account. Because it will automatically sync your last page read. Synchronization will also keep track of any bookmarks, highlights, or notes that you added, so you can view them on another device.

How to turn off? Go to "amazon.com" --- "My Account" --- "Manage Your Content and Devices" (Formerly "Manage your Kindle")--"Device

Synchronization (Whispersync Settings)". Select "Off". Everything is done!

Method 3: Share Kindle Fire ebooks with friends by lending out

1. Check that if the book is able to be lent out. Publishers decide whether books can be loaned, so not all books will be available. Look under the product details of the book on your Kindle device. If the book can be loaned out, it will say "Lending: Enabled".

2. Go to the "Actions" menu and look for the link marked "Loan this title". As long as the book can be loaned, this link will be there.

3. Click "Loan this title."Fill in the following form with the name of the other Kindle owner and her email address.

4 Click "Send now." The book will be sent to the other user. The loaned book will be available for 14 days.

5 Click on the button "Get your loaned book now" on the Kindle receiving the book.

6 Choose the device you want the book to be put in and click "Accept."

Method 4: Share Kindle books with Kindle Family Library

There is another easier and more convenient way for us to share our Kindle books, Amazon enables us share apps, books and audiobooks with family or friends. No need to lending out or share the same Amazon account.

We can set family library on our Kindle device, or set this online. Here I will introduce how to set it from Amazon official website, if you don't have a Kindle eReader or Kindle Fire device, you can still have access to it online.

1. Enter Amazon official website, hover "Your Account"   -->"Manage Your   Content   and Devices", sign in with your Amazon account. Then   click   "Settings",   you   can   see   the "Households and Family Library" item.

2. Click "Invite an Adult" button, then Amazon will let the invited adult enter his Amazon

account information. Let your partner sit down at your computer and input his account.

3. After you verify account, you'll have to agree to share your payment methods. It is required to enable the Family Library feature — or you can only manage "child profiles".

4. After you agree, you'll be able to choose to share which types of content with each other.

5. Now you have linked the 2 adult accounts together. If you like, you can also create up to four child profiles.

6. Amazon allows a full list of Kindle devices and app to access to the shared content, including Kindle eReaders, Kindle Fire tablets, as well as Kindle app for iPhone, iPad, Android, Win, Mac and the web. You can see the shared content from your partner's library under "Manage Your Content and Devices".

Note: To see the shared content on device, the option may not be enabled by default. If you cannot see the content on device, you have to click "Manage Your Content and Devices"->"Your Devices", select each device. And check "Show (Partner Name)'s content" box under Family Library for each. Your partner have to do this for their devices on their own account, too.

How to free up storage space

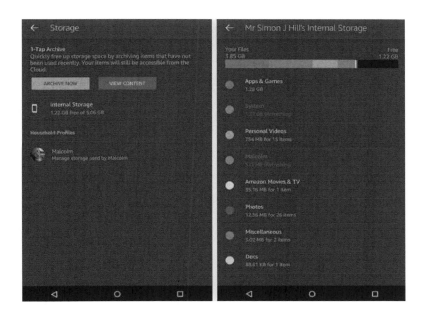

You may find that you run short on storage space after having your Fire tablet for a while, especially if you use it to take photos or shoot video. If you want to check on how much storage you have, go to **Settings** > **Storage**.

If you tap on Internal Storage, you'll get a detailed breakdown of what's on your tablet. You can go into each category, and choose to delete files to free up additional space.

You can also free up some space by offloading items you haven't used in a while under the **1-Tap Archive** option. Tap **View Content** to review the candidates for archiving and **Archive Now** to go ahead and do it. If you need to get the items back, you can always tap on them to download them again from the cloud.

How to back up photos and videos

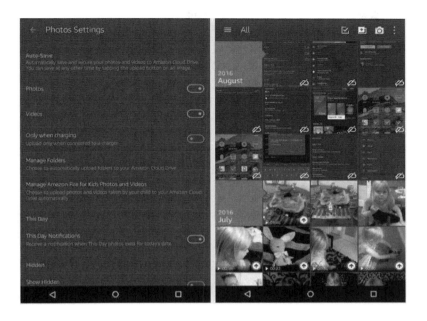

To preserve your memories and keep the photos and videos you take with your Fire tablet safe, you can automatically back them up to Amazon Drive. Every customer gets 5GB for free, but Prime members also enjoy free unlimited photo storage.

If you want to turn on the automatic backup option, then go to the Photos app, tap to expand the menu via the three horizontal lines in the top left, and choose *Settings*. You'll see separate options to turn *Auto-Save* on for Photos and Videos. You can also choose which files you'd like to back up, choose to only back up when your Fire tablet is plugged in and charging, and manage the backup for your child's profile if you have one set up on the device.

When a photo or video has not been backed up, it will have a wee icon of a cloud with a line through it in the bottom-right corner. If there's an arrow, then the file is currently uploading. When photos and videos have been backed up, you can access them in any browser by visiting *Amazon Cloud Drive* and signing in with your Amazon account.

How to filter out blue light

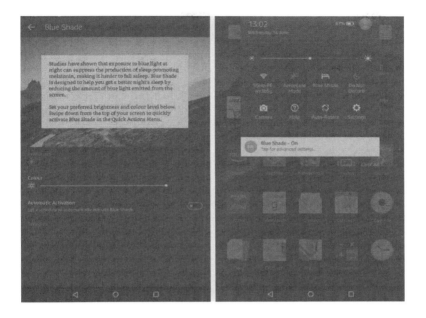

There's evidence that blue light can keep you up at night, but Amazon has included a handy feature called Blue Shade that filters out the blue light from your Fire Tablet display. To enable the feature, swipe down from the top and tap the *Blue Shade* icon. You'll see a notification that it's turned on, and your screen color will change. Tap the notification to adjust the color. There's also an option to set up Automatic Activation, so that Blue Shade turns on by itself when it's late at night, and turns off again during the day.

How to browse the web privately

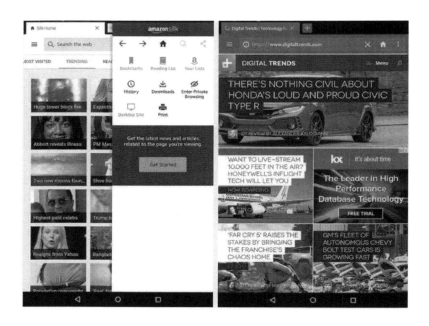

If you'd prefer that a certain browsing session didn't make its way into your history, then you need to use Silk's Private Browsing mode. To do so, tap the three vertical dots in the upper-right of the web browser and select Enter Private Browsing. When you're in Private Browsing mode, the pages you visit are not recorded in your browser history, but remember that your internet provider and the websites you visit can still view your browsing habits. You can tell when you're in Private Browsing mode at a glance, because the Silk background becomes a darker color.

How to close all tabs at once

You can close tabs one at a time in the Silk browser by tapping the "X" in the upper-right corner, but did you know that if you tap and hold "X" you can bring up an option to **Close all tabs** simultaneously? This is ideal for cleaning up after a marathon browsing session.

How to get browsing recommendations

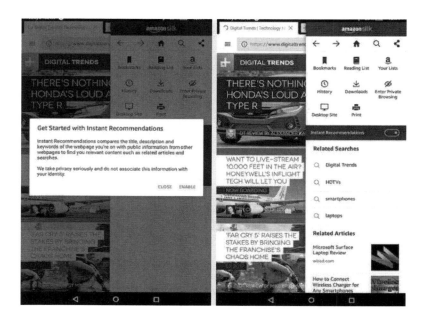

The Silk browser has a nifty feature called Instant Recommendations, which serves up related searches and articles based on the webpage you're currently visiting. Tap the three vertical dots in the upper-right corner to open the menu, where you can then turn **Instant Recommendations** on. Once activated, suggestions for other content and searches you might want to pursue will appear in this tab.

How to install apps from outside Amazon Appstore

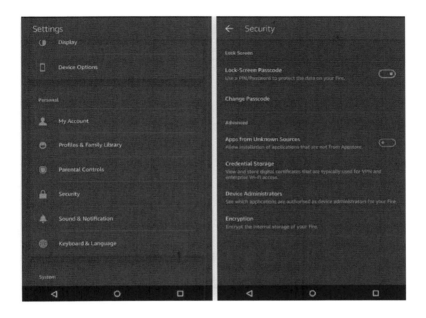

It's a shame that Fire tablets are locked into the Amazon Appstore by default because there are many more apps available in the Google Play Store and other Android app stores. Thankfully, you can load apps from other sources in a process that is known as sideloading. You will need to find the APK file, however, and get it onto your Fire tablet to install it.

To turn on the option on your Fire tablet, go to **Settings** > **Security** and toggle **Apps from Unknown Sources** on. We recommend you only do this temporarily to install an app and then toggle it off again once you're done.

There are lots of websites where you can find APK files, but you should exercise some caution because there's a lot of malware out there. *APK Mirror* is a very popular site, but stick to APK files with good reviews that have already been downloaded and used by a lot of other people. You'll also want to install an app like *ES File Explorer*. Download the APK file to your computer and plug your Fire tablet in to transfer it, or download the file directly onto your tablet via the browser. Once the download is complete, use your file explorer to find the APK file on your Fire tablet and tap on it to initiate the install.

Watch movies, but not just through Amazon

We have Amazon's movie options, which are, of

course, fully available on Fire Tablets to stream, and to purchase and download. This is wonderful, particularly for Prime members who have access to certain shows and films as part of the price of membership, but what about those of us who have a large collection of films in iTunes, or Google Play? Or those of us who have our own home videos we want to watch on the go on our tablet?

The Fire Tablet can absolutely let you watch videos outside of Amazon's interfaces, and it lets you do so easily. For those with the large iTunes, Google Play, or Vudu libraries, you can download the **Movies Anywhere** app onto your Fire Tablet to watch any of your movies, anywhere, at any time. The app even accesses Amazon, so you can find all of your movie purchases in one place.

Through Movies Anywhere, you can stream the movies you've purchased, or you can download them right to your tablet for offline viewing. With the app download, you get the ability to take advantage of many streaming and download services for film all at once, and you also get 5 free movies the first time you use the app. It's a pretty sweet deal. If you have videos downloaded to your home computer that you've made, or that are from a download service other than the ones Movies Anywhere can access.

Just connect your Fire Tablet to your computer via USB. Once you're connected, get to your Fire Tablet's storage (you might need to have a microSD card in your tablet in order for this to be accessible by your computer), and copy the video files you want into this storage space. These files have to be MP4, MKV, 3GP, M4V or WEBM format in order for the tablet to play them. When the files are all copies and you unplug your tablet, go to "**Video**" on the tablet, and then "**Library**," and tap the menu in the corner. You should find the files you transferred under the category **"Personal Videos,"** and you'll be able to watch them on the go at your leisure.

You can also watch through apps like Netflix and HBO Now on your Fire Tablet, and Netflix will even let you download episodes and movies for offline viewing. So that's another way to watch non-Amazon things on your Fire Tablet, but accessing non-Amazon movie libraries might be the most surprising method, and the most useful, for those of us who've built up movie libraries in multiple places.

10 tips to make the most of Alexa on your Amazon Fire tablet

Amazon Alexa is a voice-activated personal assistant that can answer questions and perform a growing number of actions. First used on Amazon Echo smart speakers, Alexa can check the weather or traffic, set alarms or reminders, make lists, provide news briefings, play music or audiobooks, tell jokes, or even sings songs.

The personal assistant was available on Amazon Fire tablets since September 2016, when the 6th-generation HD 8 was launched. But it's the introduction of Fire HD 10 in 2017 when Alexa's benefits fully met possibilities of Amazon Fire tablets. It was the first model that enabled owners to use Alexa without touching the screen, turning their tablet into a fully-fledged Echo Show speaker – or much more.

In the list below, you will learn how to enable hands-free Alexa (and why it's good to do it), or how to make the most of Show Mode. We focus on visually-enhanced Alexa skills and commands, plus answer most common questions about using Alexa on the Fire tablet.

Alexa on Amazon Fire tablets – tips and facts

1. Use Alexa hands-free

Did you know you can use Alexa on your Fire tablet without touching its screen? If you bought the Fire model released in 2017 or later, you can start using hands-free Alexa right away.

Hands-free Alexa was introduced together with Amazon Fire HD 10 in September 2017. In April 2018, Amazon brought it to the 7th-generation Fire 7 and HD 8 via the software update. Older models won't get Alexa hands-free mode, though.

What's so special about hands-free Alexa? Before, you had to press the home button to enable Alexa and ask for weather, check upcoming events, or play an audiobook. Now, you can do it from a distance. You don't even have to be anywhere near the tablet. Say "Alexa," wait for the activation sound, and ask a question or give a command.

How to enable hands-free Alexa

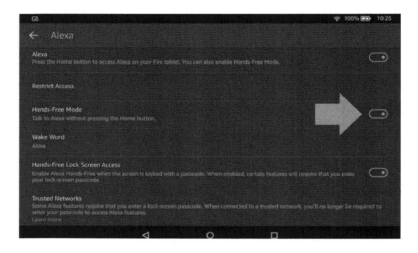

- On your Fire tablet, go to Settings (in the Home view, look for the gear icon).
- In the "Device" section, find Alexa, and tap it.
- Find "Hands-Free Mode," and tap a toggle switch next to it.

2. Turn your Amazon Fire into Echo Show

Alexa is a voice-activated personal assistant, but it's not about sound any longer. Echo Show, Amazon's top-shelf Alexa-powered smart speaker equipped with the 7-inch display, can provide both audio and video replies. For

84

instance, you can watch news briefing from Reuters or CNN, see your recent photos, make video calls, or read music lyrics.

With hands-free Alexa, you don't have to buy Echo Show or Echo Spot (the smaller speaker with the 2.5-inch screen). The Fire tablet, if you purchased the 7th-generation or later model, can do that as well.

Use the Fire together with Show Mode Charging Dock

Show Mode Charging Dock is a $39 accessory specifically designed to make the full use of hands-free Alexa and Show Mode on your Fire tablet. The accessory consists of two parts: the backshell case and the charging dock. It enables you to switch your Fire from being hand-operated to voice-operated by merely placing it on the charging stand.

When you put the Fire on the stand:

- the Show Mode automatically turns on,
- the Fire is being charged via metal connectors at the bottom of the dock – there is no need to plug the cable.

You can change the angle of the stand to reach maximum visibility across the room.

Use the Fire without Show Mode Charging Dock

You don't need to invest in a charging dock to use your Fire tablet the same way as Echo Show or Spot. If you have a stand case, you can do that as well. Just open the case and fold it to form the horizontal stand. Place is where you want it to be – but remember one thing: to enable the hands-free Alexa, the Fire has to be connected to a power source.

To place the tablet at the right angle, you can alternatively use any universal tablet stand. It doesn't have to be a tailored Amazon Fire stand case. This method is less convenient than Show Mode Charging Dock because you need to plug the cable and turn on the Show Mode manually.

On the other side, the Fire has to be charged quite often, so you'll have to do it anyway. Instead of placing it on a bedside table, form a stand and make it ready to respond to your voice commands.

3. Make the most use of Show Mode

When responding to your question or answer, Alexa can provide visual information even when Show Mode is turned off. You will see weather conditions, current time, or confirmation of the alarm being set.

But the Show Mode does it so much better. Visuals are enhanced and designed to be visible from a distance. Letters are more prominent and bolder. Longer information is being split into a sequence – everything is dedicated to achieving maximum visibility. The currently spoken passage of a longer text is being highlighted.

To see the difference, let's compare weather information.

Alexa shows weather without Show Mode

Alexa shows weather with Show Mode

The Show Mode is much more than just better-displayed information. It shows example commands you can try, so it's the easiest possible way to learn about what Alexa can do for you. When the Show Mode is on, the Fire wakes up when you are near, displaying time, weather conditions, and recent notifications.

When you enable Show Mode, the display will be automatically turned to horizontal view, overriding the setup of your choice (Auto-Rotate / Portrait / Landscape).

You can control what information you want to see while the Show Mode is on. To do that:

- In the Home view, go to Settings.
- In the "Device" section, find "Show Mode" and tap it.
- Play with the options.

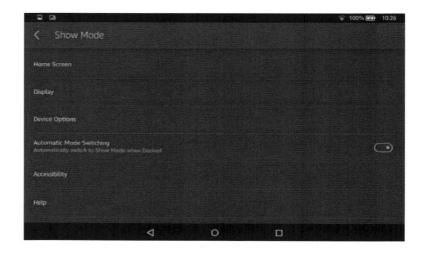

Home Screen

- Background – it lets you decide which background you see. It's either the default set of images or a slideshow from the selected photo album from your Prime account,

- Home Cards – you can decide which information you want to see: notifications from Alexa skills, upcoming events from your calendar, trending topics, new reminders.

Display

You can set here photo slideshow preferences, and decide whether to show ambient clock when the Fire is inactive.

Automatic Mode Switching

It applies to Fire tablets that are equipped with Show Mode Charging Dock. You can toggle whether you want to automatically switch to Show Mode when docked.

Accessibility

When you turn this option on, you will hear transcripts for received messages.

How to enable Show Mode on the Fire tablet

As I said before, if you use Show Mode Charging Dock, the Show Mode will be activated automatically every time you put the tablet on the charging stand.

To do it without the stand, you can choose one of the options:

- **Option 1**: say "Alexa, turn on Show Mode" or "Alexa, switch to Show Mode,"
- **Option 2**: swipe down from the top of the screen to reveal Quick Action menu, and switch Show Mode toggle located below the controls and above the notifications.

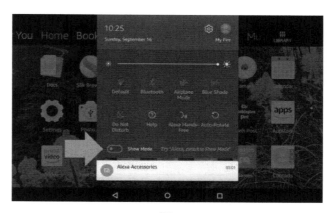

To disable Show Mode

You can do it using one of three methods:

- **Option 1**: say "Alexa, exit Show Mode,"
- **Option 2**: swipe down from the top of the screen to reveal Quick Action menu, and switch Show Mode toggle,
- **Option 3**: unplug the Fire from the power source (7th-generation Fire 7 and Fire HD 8).

4. Use Alexa to read your Kindle books

One of the most popular Alexa features is the ability to play Audible audiobooks. However, there is another, completely free way to listen to a book, and you don't even need to add an audiobook companion to a previously bought Kindle title.

Alexa can simply activate the text-to-speech function in the Kindle app. Obviously, it will work for you if you can stand a mechanical Alexa voice for a longer time.

To start listening to a Kindle book, say:

Alexa, play the Kindle book, (title).

To continue listening to a Kindle book, say:

Alexa, resume my Kindle book.

Try also other commands:

Alexa, pause / skip / stop my Kindle book.

At any time, you can ask Alexa to adjust the reading by using one of the following commands:

Alexa, read louder.
Alexa, stop reading in 15 minutes.
Alexa, next chapter.

You can play any book from the Kindle Store that supports text-to-speech technology. Alexa can also read books that you get via Amazon subscription: Kindle Unlimited or Amazon Prime

(Kindle Owners' Lending Library and Amazon Prime Reading).

Alexa can read Kindle books in one of the following languages:

- English (US, UK, CA, AU, IN)
- German
- Japanese

How to check out if text-to-speech is available for the Kindle book

- In your web browser, go to the Kindle Store and find a book you want to check out,
- Scroll down the page to reveal "Product details" section,
- Look for "Text-to-Speech" option and make sure it says "Enabled."

Product details

File Size: 1806 KB
Print Length: 526 pages
Publisher: Lake Union Publishing (May 1, 2017)
Publication Date: May 1, 2017
Sold by: Amazon Digital Services LLC
Language: English
ASIN: B01L1CEZ6K
Text-to-Speech: Enabled
X-Ray: Enabled
Word Wise: Enabled
Lending: Not Enabled
Screen Reader: Supported
Enhanced Typesetting: Enabled
Amazon Best Sellers Rank: #86 Paid in Kindle Store (See Top 100 Paid in Kindle Store)
> #1 in Kindle Store > Kindle eBooks > Literature & Fiction > Historical Fiction > **Italian**
> #2 in Kindle Store > Kindle eBooks > Literature & Fiction > Literary Fiction > **Biographical**
> #4 in Books > Literature & Fiction > Genre Fiction > **Biographical**

5. If you start with Alexa, stop with Alexa

Amazon Fire is not a single-purpose device like the Echo. Alexa is just one of the ways to use it. If you don't want to get confused, try to stop using the Fire the way you started it. If you used Alexa to start an audiobook playback, use Alexa to stop it. Otherwise, you may encounter unexpected behavior.

Alexa handles actions independently from apps. If it reads a Kindle book, it doesn't mean it opens the Kindle app to read it. Therefore, if you ask Alexa to read a Kindle book, don't be surprised that opening a Kindle app to stop text-to-speech will not take effect. Because the Kindle app "doesn't know" that Alexa is reading the book for you. It's even more evident with an Audible audiobook. If you trigger an audiobook playback with Alexa and decide to stop it by opening the Audible app, you may end up playing the same audiobook twice.

How to stop Alexa – Show Mode off

If you use the Fire tablet without the Show Mode, you can stop Alexa in one of the following ways:

- **Option 1**: say "Alexa, stop / pause,"
- **Option 2**: tap the Close icon in the top right corner of the screen,
- **Option 3**: slide down from the top edge of the display to reveal the Quick Action menu. In the notifications section, there is a currently opened Alexa action. Tap the Play / Pause button and/or slide it to the

left.

How to stop Alexa – Show Mode on

Use one of the following ways:

- **Option 1**: say "Alexa, stop / pause,"
- **Option 2**: slide down from the top edge of the display to reveal the Quick Action menu. In the notifications section, there is a currently opened Alexa action. Slide it to the left.

6.   Make   the most   of   Alexa's   visual responses

On a smart speaker, Alexa can give you only an audio response. It's much more fun when the display comes into play.

There is a growing number of Alexa features and skills that display visual content. You can watch Flash Briefings, make video calls, watch videos on Amazon Prime Video, or preview photos from your Prime Photos account.

All basic features provided by Alexa come with full visual responses, as well. Setting the alarm or timer, viewing upcoming events, adding new items to a shopping list – you will not only hear but also see them.

One of the most helpful Alexa features on the Fire tablet are video Flash Briefings. If you enable one of the briefings that are enhanced with video, you can start watching the latest news on your Fire by saying:

Alexa, show me CNN News / Fox News / NBC News

How to enable video-enhanced Alexa Flash Briefings

By default, your Flash Briefing on the Fire tablet is Reuters Now. You can add other networks as well, and control the order. To enable video-enhanced Alexa news services:

- Go to the Home screen of your Fire tablet

and open the Amazon Alexa app (the light blue icon).

- Tap the menu icon in the top left corner, find "Things to Try," and tap it.
- Swipe down to reveal the "News" section. Tap it.
- Swipe down to the bottom of the screen. Under "Explore More" you will see "Discover News Skills" – tap it to open the Amazon Alexa Skills section featuring Flash Briefing with full video support.

Top video-enhanced Alexa News Skills

- Reuters TV (US and World)
- People
- The Tonight Show Monologue

7. Avoid lock screen passcode when using hands-free Alexa

Some users set a lock screen passcode to protect sensitive data on their Fire tablet. When you enable hands-free Alexa, you will not be required to enter the PIN only when asking for general information, such as Flash Briefing or weather. Every time you ask Alexa to provide personal information, such as upcoming calendar events, you will be required to enter the lock screen passcode.

One way to avoid the lock screen passcode with Alexa is disabling it in the Fire's Settings. But there is a better way. You can still have your Fire password protected but use freely with hands-free Alexa at home.

How to use hands-free Alexa at home without the passcode

Go to the Home screen of your Fire tablet, and open Settings. In the "Device" section, tap "Alexa." Here, there are two things to do:

- **Step 1**: On a list, find "Hands-Free Lock Screen Access." Make sure it's turned on.

- **Step 2**: Right below, you will find another setting – "Trusted Networks." Tap it, and then tap "Add Trusted Network." On a list of available or saved Wi-Fi networks, find the one that's yours. Tap it and confirm your selection.

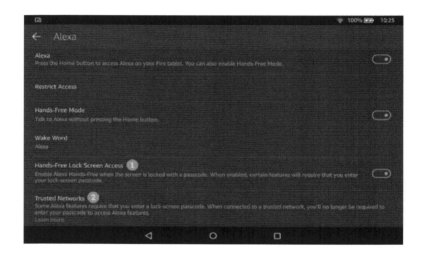

8. Use Amazon Alexa app to discover commands and skills

I said earlier that the Show Mode is the easiest and most natural way to learn about possibilities Alexa gives the Amazon Fire user. If you would like to embrace Alexa faster, you can use the

Amazon Alexa app for that.

The app enables the user to control a few more settings, such as managing preferences for Alexa features (music, TV schedules, Flash Briefings, and more).

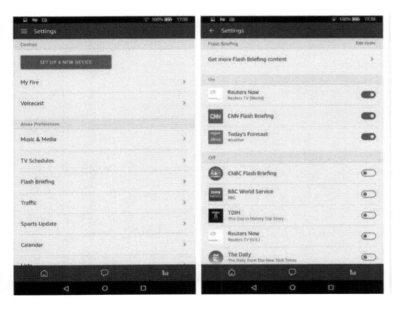

However, the most important benefit of the app is that it shows how to use Alexa – which commands to use to achieve the desired result.

When you tap the app's menu in the top left

corner, you will see a long list of items. An item you have to check out is "Things To Try." You will find here example Alexa commands in a number of areas, such as:

- What's New
- Sports
- Questions & Answers
- News
- Smart Home
- Routines
- Reminders
- Messaging

9. Use Alexa to set up a routine

Many people have daily routines. Are you among those who check out the weather, news headlines, and local traffic when eating breakfast? Amazon Fire can provide that multi-step information for you, and all you should do is say one Alexa command.

It's possible, thanks to a feature called "Routines," available in the Amazon Alexa app. It lets you perform a sequence of actions.

How to create an Alexa routine on the Fire tablet

- Open Amazon Alexa app and tap the menu icon in the top left corner.
- On the list of available items, find "Routines" – tap it.

Now you are in the section, where you can either enable/disable the routines or create your own one. One routine is already there, so the only thing to do is to enable it. The routine, triggered by "Alexa, start my day," provides the following sequence of actions:

- tell you something new
- provide weather information
- report traffic
- play the news

You can change the order, remove items, or add

new elements to the routine. Then, switch the toggle in the top right corner to enable the routine and test it!

You can also create a routine from scratch. Go one step back and tap "Create Routine" button. Have fun!

10. Alexa on the Fire tablet – quick questions and answers

Find below the most common questions regarding using Alexa and Show Mode on Amazon Fire tablet.

Q: What is Show Mode?

A: Show Mode is a special interface on Amazon Fire tablets that enhances Alexa with visual information.

Q: How do I get new Alexa skills?

A: Open Amazon Alexa app, then Menu, then Skills & Games. Obviously, you can always ask: "Alexa, suggest new skills."

Q: Can I change the wake word?

A: Yes,... sort of. The only other option you can select is "Amazon." There is no way to set a custom wake word.

Q: Is there is a monthly fee on Alexa?

A: No, Alexa is a free service provided by Amazon.

Thank you for purchasing our book, we believed you learned a lot of tips and tricks that will help you master your new Fire 7 tablet.

Printed in Great Britain
by Amazon